Preface

My father had Alzheimer's disease. I was the primary caregiver for him. Four and one- half years I cared for him in my home; two and one-half more years I spent being the watchful eye of the care he was given in long-term care facilities.

Dementia is not a disease; the symptoms are the clues the doctors use to determine the disease. I was told the most common cause of dementia is Alzheimer's. That is a very hard diagnosis for doctors to make because Alzheimer's disease is confirmed by an autopsy.

There were many tests my father went through that led the doctors to their diagnosis. He had many other health issues besides the loss of memory and behavioral problems.

There are so many stages everyone has to go through in a situation like this—the person with the disease and those caring for them. Many changes take place in the home of the caregiver, and they affect family, friends and relatives, adults and children alike. It is a life-changing experience for everyone.

I know I was extremely resentful that very few of my family members lent a helping hand and not as often as I needed. How dare everyone just expect me to put my life on hold while they continued on with theirs as though nothing had changed. Anger and bitterness were very hard for me to keep in control.

Alzheimer's disease has several stages. You do not die of it; you die with it. It is hard to recognize the early signs of Alzheimer's disease unless you are very familiar with the person. Because the changes are not consistent every day and come on so gradually, they can be confused with aging or health problems. But there comes a time when the person can no longer make it on his own.

My father had become disoriented and was lost for 18 hours. He had been traveling on a bus and did not know where his stop was.

Can you imagine what it would be like to be disoriented in a strange city after dark? What a panic he must have been in, trying to remember where he was supposed to be. He was found outside a hotel, in a corner, huddled up behind some bushes, scared half out of his mind. He could have been robbed, gotten in the way of traffic, or fallen to his death.

I did not seek a caregiver's group though I should have. I struggled through those years doing the best I could. I felt very inadequate for the most part unless guilt took over, and believe me, the feeling of inadequacy was by far more desirable than the feelings of guilt. I didn't like either one of them.

Then came the day I could no longer take care of my father at home. I would never have believed that overseeing his care elsewhere was going to be so much harder to handle than caring for him at home. At least I knew what was going on while he was with me. There were times I thought I was losing my mind I was so mentally exhausted.

I cannot tell you how many others I know who have entered into the caregiver's role since my experience. I have tried to encourage them to find someone who will listen to their concerns.

Because this book has not been easy to put together and I've been struggling with it for almost six years, I can honestly say I would have given up on it long ago had it not been for the commitment I made to write it.

Recently a very dear friend of mine and I were talking. I was struggling with how to end this book, and she asked me, "What are you trying to say and why do you feel the need to say it?" Well, that was way too many hard questions for me to answer all in a row.

It would be by far easier for me to stand in front of a stadium full of people and tell this than to have to put it on paper, in sentences that will make sense and be interesting enough for the reader not to want to put it down until they have finished it, and then say, "OH NO! What happened next?"

Well, let me help you decide if you want to even read the first chapter by answering those very hard questions my friend asked me. "What is the purpose of writing this book?" All I know is, I needed help and couldn't find it no matter where I looked or to whom I looked. So the answer to that question would be to help others find help and to know where to look for help. "Who are you trying to reach?" I am trying to reach anyone and everyone who is looking for the answers. The last question was "What are you trying to say and why do you feel the need to say it?" I am trying to say that the answer was right there in front of me, but I failed to recognize it. My hope is to show you how to find the answers, because it was those answers that gave me the help and hope I needed to get me through that trying time.

That same friend told me I would have to start at the very beginning, so that is where I will start.

Dedication

To my husband for allowing me to tell the story the way it was then, and the way it is now.

To the Alzheimer's Association for their continuing and relentless research on this dreadful disease.

To my family and friends who were so forgiving when I was in the heat of the battle.

To everyone who encouraged and endured with me through the writing of this book.

Contents

Chapter 1. 13
In the Beginning

Chapter 2. 19
Follow Me and We'll Go Places

Chapter 3. 28
Isn't That Just A Filthy Piece of Coal?

Chapter 4. 39
I Promise You, Lord

Chapter 5. 47
The Pruning of My Orchard

Chapter 6. 59
Thanks, Lord, But No Thanks

Chapter 7. 69
Is That You, Lord?

Chapter 8. 74
Can You Wait a Minute, Lord, I Have to Dust!

Chapter 1

In the Beginning

"It's another girl!" I can only imagine my father's disappointment at the doctor's announcement. I was the second daughter, with two more following in the next two years. My mother had some sort of health issue, then there was "the surgery," and there would be no more babies at our house. He wanted a boy, as most men do, and the hope of that was forever lost. My mother was excommunicated from our church because of the surgery, and my father was not happy about that either, which could explain why we girls were allowed to go to church but our parents never went with us.

My paternal grandparents lived across the street from us, and it was on their dining room table that I was born. Maybe that's why I'm hungry all the time!

My father worked for the family landscaping business, which had government contracts to clear the way for telephone lines in several states. That meant he was home only a few days a month. In 1953 a tree limb fell on my father's head and broke his neck, which necessitated his staying home to recuperate. He was scary to us girls because we hardly knew him, and I have no doubt his serving in the Navy during

World War II was the reason he expected immediate willing obedience—or else! I was four years old, had been on the other end of "OR ELSE," and was not the least bit fond of it. I tried to respond immediately, but that didn't always work out. He never did seem kind or gentle, and we tried to stay out of his way because he was abusive, both mentally and physically.

We lived in Iowa, a beautiful state that I shall never forget. Fall and winter months were, and still are, my favorites. I loved living there and have so many wonderful memories. In the fall, the leaves on the tree-lined streets were so beautiful. I loved the sound and smell as I walked through them going to school and church. Back in those days, people would burn leaves, and I loved that smell, too. Even to this day, that smell brings back so many wonderful memories. Every winter I spent most of my time inside, looking out, watching it either rain or snow.

I had health problems as a child and missed weeks of school at a time in the winter months from kindergarten through the third grade. I wanted to go to school, but as a sickly little crybaby, I had to stay home and, consequently, fell behind in reading, writing and arithmetic. And I can assure you, I never won a spelling bee either.

When I was able to return to school, I was be behind in class work and confused. Everyone seemed to know all the answers, and I never did. They seemed to know all the other kids, and I knew just a few. So I was lost and uncertain most of the time. I wanted my mom and thought she was probably home coloring without me.

In April of 1959, my father's stepfather died. The family business was sold, along with the house in which we lived. I was so sad and confused as I watched all our belongings being sold at an auction and could hardly believe we had to move to Arizona. At the age of nine, "new" was not that exciting to me. I did not want anything to change if it meant leaving behind anyone or anything I loved. Luckily for me, my mom and sisters were coming, too. My father had gone ahead of us, so we would be traveling on our own.

Mom hadn't been driving many years, so we were in for a real adventure. I do not remember all the details of that trip, but there were "details." Old car, bad tires, pulling a trailer with a car full of kids, little money—get the picture? My father had marked our course on an old, faded map. With that as our only guide, we left all but a few necessities behind and headed for Arizona.

My mother was very courageous to endure the three-day journey that took us four days to complete. I am sure we spent a lot of time lost because of the unexpected detours and new roads that were not on that old map. I do remember the dim dome light coming on more than once as Mom and my twelve-year-old sister tried to determine where Mom had made the wrong turn and how many miles we would have to backtrack to get headed in the right direction again.

We slept in the car and ate on the side of the road. This was the adventurous part, to us at least. My poor mother must have made a lot of mistakes though, because she heard about what she should have done for a very long time after that.

Unfortunately, we had no place to live once we got to Arizona. However, we met two of the most fabulous people in the world who opened up their home to us. We stayed with them until we found a place of our own, and they ended up being lifelong friends of our whole family. Friends like that are so very, very important and very, very hard to come by.

Arizona wasn't beautiful. It couldn't even be classified as pretty. Our first Christmas was so hot that we went swimming! What a big difference compared to making snowmen. There was no holiday spirit, and it was way too hot to think it could be Christmas time.

Things had changed all right, but I still wanted to go home. I longed for all that was familiar to me. My mother used to say, "Home is where the heart is." Well this was not it. My heart was back in Iowa. Feeling as lost as I could feel, I understood there would be no going back. We were "home." The older I got, the meaner my father got. For some reason, he hated his mother. In spite of what he said about her, I would never hate her. In all the years of his life, I never heard him say one nice thing about her, or to her for that matter. I knew my grandparents were wealthy, and money had a lot to do with the growing hatred he had toward her.

Of course, children are never filled in with all the details of the lives of their parents. For instance, I did not know that my father had been born out of wedlock. Back in the 1920s, this was a big shame to the family. His maternal grandmother raised him until the age of ten years old, so I am sure he felt abandoned by his mother.

Most of his anger possibly came from the feeling of not being accepted by anyone, even those at his grandmother's church. He always thought the people there treated his grandmother wrong even though she attended that church faithfully. Those thoughts were probably confirmed when the pastor of the church sent a stranger to conduct her funeral and no one from the church came to pay their last respects.

After her death, my father went to live with his mother and her husband. There were three children born to them, but one was a "blue baby" and died just days after her birth. He watched as his mother mourned the baby's death, yet she had willingly walked away from him.

The half-sister and half-brother were the constant main attraction and had rooms upstairs while he was given a space in the basement. He felt like an outsider and blamed his mother for it all. How incredibly sad it must have been for a ten-year-old boy to lose the only one he knew loved him, then to have to live with someone he felt had abandoned him. This also could explain why he didn't go to church with us girls.

Four years after moving to Arizona, we still lived in a one-bedroom house. In the meantime, my grandmother sold the remaining properties, two other businesses, her furs, jewelry and all but one car. She spent every single cent through squander and waste. Again she was living on the same street as we were only this time it wasn't the nicest house. I was glad to have her back, but she didn't stay long.

More years went by, and though it didn't seem like it at the time, they went by very fast. In 1965 I found myself standing in the office of the justice of the peace, my mother at my side, as I said, "I do." I was now married! It didn't matter to me that I had not finished high school. All I really wanted was to be a wife and mother. Now I didn't have to live in the same house with my father, and life was going to be so different. Different it was. Oh, the heartache I put my parents through.

In November of 1965, our first son was born, and our little family moved to California. In September of 1967 our second son was born. Our third son was born in March of 1970, and my husband didn't want to be married anymore. Great! Now what was I going to do without a job or an education, with three small children and no money?

As I left my father's house just five years before, he told me I was on my own. I would not be moving back into his house with a batch of kids for him to raise. Knowing he meant it and not wanting to go there anyway, I wondered what I would do. I felt so lost! This was the beginning of the off-again, on-again relationship with my husband for the next six years.

I filed for divorce, hoping against all hope that this might wake him up and he would see what he would be losing. Begging hadn't worked, but maybe this would. Though I filed in 1970, I did not sign the final papers.

My grandmother came to live in California too, and we had such a good time together, but before long she left to live with her younger son and his family. My dearly beloved grandmother drank. I had heard stories from my father that she was a "closet" drinker. I had only seen her under the influence a few times, and it wasn't in a closet. This particular day it was in her living room.

I listened only out of politeness, yet I remember the conversation as if it took place yesterday. For the most part, as she was telling me about the "money" and waving a small savings account book in my face, I tried to figure out my escape. I thought all the money had been spent, not realizing at the time that the savings account was still valid and holding big bucks. When she said, "If I can't have the money, nobody can," it sounded like the bottle was talking. I didn't believe it, nor did I care. In my opinion, they were slurred words which were none of my business. She died in June of 1972, taking with her all she knew about the savings account. I was glad my father went to her funeral. I didn't think it was possible. But now he was bitterer than ever.

Over the years, I developed a better relationship with my father. He and my mother loved their little grandsons and wanted to spend as much time with them as they could. In fact, in 1971 we all (including my husband, who quit his job of almost five years) returned to Arizona. I still had not signed the final divorce papers.

Our relationship went from bad to worse. In March of 1974, my husband moved to California and got his old job back. That June, I moved to California to be with him. A year later I went back to Arizona without him. This would be the last time. He sent me a telegram July 1, 1976, asking if I would sign the final papers, as he wanted to marry someone else! I wanted to say "NO!" but I knew from past experiences, you cannot make reality out of hopes, wishes or dreams. So, I signed the papers. When I married a second time, my mother and father were at my side.

Chapter 2

Follow Me and We'll Go Places

I thought I was headed in the right direction and had most of my life mapped out. Turns out I was wrong. So there you have it. I was lost the whole time. I was always lost, literally. I could have used a cell phone back in the '60s when I first started driving. With two small babies and a very undependable car, even if I found a pay phone and the nickel to call my husband, I couldn't because we didn't have a phone at home. Plus, if I didn't know where I was, how was he going to give me directions?

By the way, did you know that imitation is the sincerest form of flattery? Satan is very good at it. He has to put forth his best first, but even his best cannot, nor will it ever, produce eternal life with God in Heaven. It will be eternal life all right, but it will be with him in Hell. Do not be fooled by Satan.

God's Word has warned us to beware of false teachers and preachers. They are imitators of God's Word. They add to or take away and maybe even rearrange it so it sounds very similar, but will fit their sinful life. Satan has to do that so you will never see the need for Christ in your life. ***Matthew 7:15*** says, ***"Beware of false prophets, which come to you in*** *sheep's clothing, but inwardly they are ravening wolves."* Verse 16 says, *"Ye shall know them by their fruits."* Satan is not the real thing like he wants you to believe. He is real, but he is "the wolf in sheep's clothing."

We need to do as it says in *2 Timothy 2:15, 16: "Study to shew thyself approved unto God, a workman that needeth not to be ashamed, rightly dividing the word of truth. But shun profane and vain babblings: for they will increase unto more ungodliness."* False doctrine will keep you in Hell for eternity! No belief, no faith, no strength! You can know for sure if you are going to Heaven, I mean, know for sure if Heaven is your home.

In the '70s I had a better car, a phone and a job. Otherwise, things weren't much better. I was still always getting lost. Even if I could have found a phone and the dime, I couldn't have called my husband because of the divorce. So I was lost and divorced with three kids.

Did you know that God seeks us first? Truthfully, those Bible thumping, born-again Christians and their fanatical ways annoyed me. There was one in my ex-husband's family. A cousin, well acquainted with the drink, found in a desperate condition, broke, virtually kicked to the curb, and lying in his own vomit, got saved and became a born-again Christian.

I had heard strange things about the "born-again." I did not want them bothering me at my door, on the phone, in line or out of line. Just leave me alone! After all, remember, I had my life all mapped out. So the map had a few wrinkles in it. I was still on my way to Hell, and I didn't even know it. Yikes!

I had heard about God and believed all the things I had heard. I knew about the baby Jesus. I knew about His mother Mary. I even bowed down to her during my younger years. I had heard the story about the Wise Men and the presents they gave and how they followed a star to find Him. Alrighty then! I was a good person! I had heard that God was very loving and forgiving and so forth and so on, and I just figured I would be going to Heaven. I hadn't read ***John 14:6*** where Jesus said, *"... **I am the way, the truth, and the life: no man cometh unto the Father, but by me.**"* Or ***Romans 3:10-12:*** *"...**There is none righteous,** [good] **no, not one: There is none that understandeth, there is none that seeketh after God. They are all gone out of the way, they, they are together become unprofitable; there is none that doeth good, no, not one.**"*

This means that not one of us in this world is the exception, not even me. But wait a minute! I was good. After all, I was not a murderer or the biggest liar I knew, nor was I a major thief, and I could explain it all away on the day I entered into Heaven. However, I was young and did not give much thought to death. I would deal with all that when the time came. It wasn't that time, and I had dinner to make, kids to feed, and the house to clean before the next Bible thumpers came along. What did they know anyway? I could talk to God anytime I wanted. There were so many different religions out there. Who knew for sure which was the one God was in? The church I had attended when I was young didn't even speak in English. I could never figure out what they were talking about, and the nuns were mean.

Of course, I thought I deserved to go to Heaven. In fact, I never even worried about not going because I knew I was a good person. I could not have been more wrong. This was not a matter of what I thought about me, nor about how good I had been or could be, or about how wonderful my friends thought I was. It was about what God already knew about me.

I didn't know we could never be good enough nor do enough good things to earn our way to Heaven. ***Ephesians 2:8, 9*** says, *"**For by grace are ye saved through faith; and*** *that not of yourselves: it is the gift of God: Not of works, lest any man should boast."*

The word *grace* means "unmerited favor, not deserved but given anyway." According to **Hebrews 11:1:** *"Now faith is the substance of things hoped for, the evidence of things not seen."* Of course, a gift is something given to you by someone, and you will never have to pay for it. You will not have to earn it; it will cost you nothing, but you do have to accept it for it to be yours. To God be the glory. He gets all the credit for your getting into Heaven. It is only because of His love for us. ***John 3:16*** say, ***"For God so loved the world, that he gave his only begotten Son, that whosoever believeth in him should not perish, but have everlasting life."***

In the early '80s, my mother was in the hospital, and we all knew that she was dying. There was no doubt, no hope, and no cure. So for twenty-eight days, I sat by her side. She was my best friend in this world, and I wanted every second I could get with her. Day and night were not too much for me. I wanted to make sure she was treated right and had anything she wanted. I only went home when others came to visit. I did quick clean-ups, quick shopping, quick eating, quick everything, for I knew not the hour she would slip away. I remember when she told me the doctors wanted to do a biopsy. I nearly jumped right out of my skin! "Mom, do you know what that means? They will open up your chest. With all the coughing you do, it will be so painful. Are you sure you want to put yourself through all that?" She said it was her last hope for life, and she was taking it.

None of us had been in church for many years, not even on Christmas or Easter. I began trying to reintroduce myself to God, calling upon Him, "Oh, LORD, don't let this be happening. Please, I will do anything. Oh, please, LORD, not now." That is how I prayed until the day I went to the hospital's chapel.

She did have the biopsy, and I am sure it did not add to the few days she had left. The doctors had told us we should notify all the next of kin as soon as possible. With those words, we knew it would not be long. Mom had two sisters and three brothers whom we called right away. There were my father, the four of us girls and our families, those two fabulous lifelong friends, and my father's cousin and his wife.

The cousins were born-again Christians! Oh boy, wouldn't you just know it? One of my sisters came right out and said, "We don't want any religion, so just keep it to yourselves."

They said, "Okay," and did just that, until she was not around, and then the cousin asked me if I would mind if he went in and talked to my mother about the Lord.

I said, "If she doesn't mind, neither do I."

After the biopsy, Mom was on life support from that day forward. Consequently, she had a tube down her throat and was unable to speak. That did not keep her from writing notes, moving her lips, or giving hand signals to let us know what she wanted us to know.

When the cousin went in to visit with my mother, I went to find the hospital chapel. Not only did I feel the need to reintroduce myself to God, but I needed to do it in His house. On my knees, now praying for my mother's sake, I asked God to do whatever was best for her, no longer focusing on my selfish losses, but on her pain and suffering. Oh, how I hoped He would hear me. All I knew about God was that He was in Heaven and could see and hear everything, but I hadn't seen or heard from Him yet...

The cousin was in the families' waiting room when I came back from the chapel. He thanked me for letting him have that opportunity to speak to my mother, then told me she had accepted the LORD as her personal Savior. When I went in to see her, I sensed something different as she started

My Father In Heaven My Father On Earth

telling me she was going Home. I just agreed with her. She could tell I was not catching on. She started pointing to the ceiling. "No, mom, we are on the top floor now. They are not going to move you." I could see she was getting frustrated and I started playing the guessing game with her.

I finally got it out of her that Home was Heaven, and I wanted to know how she knew that. She mouthed, "Because Jesus told me so."

Well, then, that did it! She must be hallucinating again. The doctors said that was what was going on when she said she could see things we couldn't. Just the day before, she had been very anxious and trying to pull the tubes out. She told me many times she wanted water put on the machines because someone was trying to come through the tubes to get her. I explained that we could not put water on the machines because it would electrocute not only her, but most likely everyone in the area. Suddenly it dawned on me: she might be talking about holy water. Bingo! That's what she wanted! So I called a priest, and he came and performed what was the scariest ritual I have ever seen.

I saw what holy water really is. I watched as the priest went over to the sink at the nurses' station and put tap water in a small bottle. He didn't even say a prayer or whatever he was supposed to do to make it holy. It was just tap water. I feel sorry for those trusting in holy water. I know it didn't help my mother one single second. Her anxiety seemed to increase—that is, until she spoke with my father's cousin. She was not hallucinating about Jesus telling her so. She had a peace about her, and I wanted to know more, but she was very weak. It was at an early hour the next morning she slipped away.

I don't know exactly what part of Scripture my father's cousin used while showing her the plan of salvation as I wasn't in the room, but he said it was from the Romans Road (to salvation), so it probably sounded like this: "I have some good news for you. Would you like to hear it?" She probably nodded her head, and he proceeded. "It says in **Romans 3:23, *'For all have sinned, and come short of the glory of God;'* and Romans 6:23, *'For the wages of sin is death; but the gift of God is eternal life through Jesus Christ our Lord.'***

Romans 5:8, 9* says, *'But God commendeth his love toward us, in that while we were yet sinners, Christ died for us;' Much more then, being now justified by his blood, we shall be saved from wrath through him;' Romans 10:9, 10, 'That if thou shalt confess with thy mouth the Lord Jesus, and shalt believe in thine heart that God hath raised him from the dead, thou shalt be saved. For with the heart man believeth unto righteousness; and with the mouth confession is made unto salvation;' Romans 10:13, 'For Whosoever* [that is you and me] *shall call upon the name of the Lord shall be saved;'

I John 5:13, 'These things have I written unto you that believe on the name of the Son of God; that ye may know that ye have eternal life, and that ye may believe on the name of the Son of God;'

John 3:3, 6, '...Verily, Verily, I say unto thee, Except a man be born again, he cannot see the kingdom of God. That which is born of the flesh is flesh; and that which is born of the Spirit is spirit.' Matthew 18:3, 'And* [Jesus] *said, Verily I say unto you, Except ye be converted, and become as little children, ye shall not enter into the kingdom of heaven.' 2 Timothy 3:15, 'And that from a child thou hast known the holy scriptures, which are able to make thee wise unto salvation through faith which is in Christ Jesus." She accepted Christ, and she went Home just like she said. However, I was still lost...

My father was now alone for the first time in nearly 37 years. There would be no dinner waiting on the table for him when he got home from work. It was all up to him now:

meals, laundry, shopping, cleaning, whatever needed doing, he would be the one doing it.

For months after my mother's death, my father spent most of his time at my house or having me do things for him at his house. On the weekend, if he didn't call my sister and her husband, he would call me to meet him for coffee at a restaurant where he would talk until I felt like my head might fall off. I went because I felt so sorry for him and I knew he needed someone to just listen.

One day as I was just listening, he mentioned again about how he hated his mother because she had robbed him of so many things. The biggest subject of hatred was that she took the money that belonged to him. If only she would have given to him what had been promised, his life would have been different. He was so mad that she had wasted his money, drinking and gambling with her friends while his family was doing without, getting by on just the barest of necessities.

The phrase "the money" caught my attention. "She didn't get the money, Dad."

His head whipped around with a funny look on his face. "How do you know she didn't?"

I explained about the small black savings book and her comment, "If I can't have the money, nobody can!" I told him she had shown me the savings book, but not its contents, then listened to him almost an hour longer than usual that day while he told me of all the promises that were made to him. Because his neck was broken on the job, my father could have sued the family business, which would have been a hardship on everyone. He was promised that all medical expenses would be paid, that he would have a place to live, and that he would receive his usual salary. Plus, he would receive $40,000 if he would just trust them and let them take care of everything.

My father was named executor of my step-grandfather's will. If only my father would have followed his step-father's wishes and not handed that position over to his mother, he would have held the savings account book.

I was so caught off guard when he started naming the events that had taken place just before my step-grandfather's death. He wanted me to call the two banks involved and gave me the names of the banks and the names of the presidents of each bank. I just knew this was going to be the biggest waste of time, as if those people would still be the presidents of those banks some 23 years later. Right...

Well, I did exactly what he asked me to do, and I was shocked! Not only were they still the presidents, but they both remembered the events just the way my father said they had taken place. They not only remembered my step-grandfather and the money transactions, but both explained that the banks were very small and did not carry large amounts of cash back then. My step-grandfather wanted to withdraw $50,000 from one bank only to deposit $40,000 in the other bank, so he settled on $10,000 in cash and a $40,000 cashier's check.

One president even told me how many times my grandmother had tried to claim the money. Yes, she had the savings book, but she was not the rightful owner, so she could not get the money. The bad news was that they would not tell me who the rightful owner was, and without that savings book, nobody out of the bank knew for sure. Thus, no one got the money as far as we know. I do know for sure my father didn't, and neither did my grandmother.

Chapter 3

Isn't That Just a Filthy Piece of Coal?

For the next five years, talk about being lost! I lived some of the longest days of my life. I was used to talking to my mother every day or close to it. There was such emptiness in my life. My life's map had so many wrinkles in it that, by now, I could hardly make out the fine print. My second husband was soon to be my second ex-husband!

In 1985 my middle son joined the military, and I quit my job to move closer to my first ex-husband. I know that sounds pretty weird, but when your son tells you that he will see you in four years, that he could not possibly come home to visit you because that would make his dad feel left out, or if he went to visit his dad that would make you feel left out, I believed it was the only thing to do. I didn't even look at my Life's Map—I just did it.

As parents, the decisions we make do have lifelong effects on our children. Divorce is no exception. In fact, I believe it is the worst decision so selfishly decided upon in a marriage. We will never know the devastating effect the decision of divorce has on children coming from a broken home. But I can tell you this: at the expense of your decision, it will cost your children dearly. Mine were no exception.

When I left, I left behind my oldest son, that being his choice because he had a good job and was getting married soon. My father still lived in the area. In fact, they both worked at the same place. Remember, my first husband married a second time, and there was yet one more son for him. And the second wife was just that, a second ex-wife. I would like to say, "and we all lived happily ever after...," but not yet. Wow, so many lousy things had happened. This is not the way I had it planned at all.

Moving back to California, it was a challenge not staying lost for the rest of my life. I think I had it figured out! At least half of the miles I put on my car were lost miles. The other half would be coming and going to my real destinations. My problem was knowing where that was and how to get there. In the middle of misery, yet more misery came. My life's map feeling much more like cloth than paper, I would soon have to put it down, for the print was just a blur now.

I found a job paying not nearly as much as the one I had quit, but I did not care. I loved that job except for one thing—there was a Bible thumper on the premises! Yup! She sat right next to me, too. I absolutely adored her—if she would just leave me alone about the "WORD," as she put it. Oh, yeah, there was one more bit of good news for me. My first ex-husband's brother and sister-in-law lived nearby, attended church regularly, and invited me to come to church with them every time they saw me. Now that was annoying to say the least. I always replied with, "Not today. I have this, that and the next thing to do, but who knows? I might just go with you someday."

This went on until I wanted to snatch them both bald-headed. Well, wasn't that just great? The "born-again" were really moving in on me now! I remained friends with my first husband and his family, so I knew a lot about what had been going on with most of them. Then one day "the preacher of the family" came by the house with his mother. I had not seen either of them in years and was so glad for the visit. He was in town holding revival meetings at a local church and wanted his cousin and me to come along. It was only going to be for five nights. Great! And what a relief—just five nights.

"Well, not tonight, but maybe one night before it is all over, we will come." Oh, yeah, and can you believe it? That is the very same church my ex-brother-in-law and ex-sister-in-law attended, so they invited me to the revival, too! Truthfully, I wanted to go at least one night. I still hadn't heard "the preacher of the family" preach yet. You know, the cousin I was talking about who got saved back at the curb. I knew him before he got saved and had met his wife once, maybe twice. So I tried to talk the ex-husband into going with me. He didn't want to go the first four nights but relented, and we went the fifth night. I must tell you, I enjoyed myself so much. It was not like any church service I had ever attended. That was the night "the preacher of the family" gave his testimony.

As I said, I knew most of it, and the part I didn't know was not surprising. It fit his lifestyle, and he had my full attention. The night just flew, and before I knew it, it was time to go. Boy, I wished I had gone the four previous nights. I saw a change in him. Yes, he was different and yet "a born-again Christian!" I felt so sorry for him as he stood up in front of that room full of people and told of all the sinful things in his life—how he had been kicked out of the United States Army, told he was an undesirable, a hopeless drunk, and useless to anyone, including himself.

Talk about mental abuse. That was it, with a touch of brutality added in. He kept talking about getting saved. "If you are not saved, you can get saved tonight! Right now! Come up to the altar, and someone can show you right out of the Bible how you can know for sure you are on your way to Heaven." Okay, hold the phone. I'll not be going anywhere but home. Got to go now. Bye, bye...

I had seen and heard how the family had treated "the preacher." It really was brutal, to say the least. They would see him come in the front door, and everybody would head for the back door.

The preacher's mother and my ex-husband's mother, being sisters each living in different states, were always glad to see each other's kids. So my ex-mother-in-law might be the only one left in the room with the preacher, but she never minded. She treated him just like one of her own ten children.

"The preacher" led her to the Lord one day. I know because she told me about it. The worst part was I didn't want to hear about it. I listened but did not understand one single word of what she was telling me. However, I saw a change in her. Before she got saved, she was only too glad to pass on whatever gossip there was on anyone to everyone. That was the only flaw I saw in her to begin with, and she stopped that.

After her salvation, she never gossiped about anyone and would not listen if she thought someone else might be gossiping to her. I noticed the change, but never knew why she stopped. Probably, if I would have listened to her testimony, I might have figured it out.

I do regret not listening when she tried to tell me about her salvation—how Jesus' death paid for all her sins with the price of His blood. That just seemed too strange and unbelievable to me, even cultish. Well, that was the "born-again" for you. I would have been all ears for some interesting gossip, though.

God just kept seeking me. I went back to that church—not to every service, nevertheless I went. That is where I heard the plan of salvation given countless times. I went with my ex-in-laws, and sometimes my ex-husband's son would go too. As time went on, his son and I started going to church more regularly. Soon we were there just about every time the doors were open. Shortly thereafter, his son got saved and baptized. I began to feel that tugging on my heart. Once again all were standing, all eyes were closed, and every head was bowed. I really wanted to go to the altar, yet would not take that first step to get me there. Yikes! If I did that, everybody would know I was guilty. I mean it would be a public admission that I was a sinner. I could not possibly do that, for crying out loud. No! Absolutely not! Got to go now. Bye, bye...

Yet, I kept going back to hear more about the "WORD," as my co-worker put it. I will never forget the day I heard those same words, "If you are not sure you are on your way to Heaven but would like to know... If that is you, raise your hand. I would like to pray for you." I had heard them so many times, but pride kept me from it. This time I raised my hand.

Oh, I tell you, it was a tremendous struggle just to get my hand in the air. My head bowed, deep in my humiliation, I felt a tapping on my shoulder. I tell you the truth when I say I thought it was the hand of God! I am not sure if I screamed and jumped or just jumped. Relieved to know it was only an usher, I could breathe again. He wanted to know if I would like to go to the altar and be shown how I could know, for sure, Heaven would be my home.

I of course said, "NO, not today." Can you just believe it? I still said, "NO!" Then one day I found myself at the altar. I have no idea how I got there or why I went that time, but I was there. What now? The beginning of a new life for me is what! Right then and there, I accepted the Lord Jesus Christ as my personal savior.

John 3:16-18 says, *"For God so loved the world, that he gave his only begotten Son, that whosoever believeth* *in him should not perish, but have everlasting life. For God sent not his Son into the world to condemn the world; but that the world through him might be saved. He that believeth on him is not condemned: but he that believeth not is condemned already, because he hath not believed in the name of the only begotten Son of God."*

Well, I was a "whosoever," and I had sinned against God. The rest went on to say that if I believed in Jesus, I would not perish, but have everlasting life. The best part was that God did not send his Son to condemn me but to save me. (I was a sinner, already condemned because I had not accepted Jesus yet!)

I did believe and accepted the Lord Jesus as MY VERY OWN PERSONAL SAVIOR. Now I am saved, adopted, a joint heir with Jesus, a child of God! Born again a new creature in Christ! *Second Corinthians 5:17* says, *"Therefore if any man be in Christ, he is a new creature: old things are passed away; behold, all things are become new."*

Jesus' death on the Cross was full payment for my sins—past, present and future. Yes, even the ones I had not yet committed. The only sin that could have sent me to Hell, the "unpardonable sin," was now taken care of once and for all. The blaspheming of the Holy Ghost, the rejection of Jesus Christ the Son of God, is the "unpardonable sin." *Matthew 12:30-32* says, *"He that is not with me is against me; and he that gathereth not with me scattereth abroad. Wherefore I say unto you All manner of sin and blasphemy shall be forgiven unto men: but the blasphemy against the Holy Ghost shall not be forgiven unto men. And whosoever speaketh a word against the Son of man, it shall be forgiven him: but whosoever speaketh against the Holy Ghost, it shall not be forgiven him, neither in this world, neither in the world to come."*

The acceptance of Jesus Christ as your personal Savior is the only way to *Heaven*. *John 14:6* says, *"Jesus saith unto him, I am the way, the truth, and the life: no man cometh unto the Father, but by me."* Romans 14:11 tells us, *"For it is written, as I live, saith the Lord, every knee shall bow to me, and every tongue shall confess to God."* Ephesians 2:8, 9 says, *"For by grace are ye saved through faith; and that not of yourselves: it is the gift of God: Not of works, lest any man should boast."* Now I understood why I could not work or buy my way to Heaven, how my good works could never outweigh the bad things I had done.

The void I had with the loss of my mother is no longer there. I am so glad that my father's cousin did not listen to my sister when she told him to keep his religion to himself and that he was bold enough, in the Lord, to give the plan of salvation to my mother just hours before her death.

You see, I know my mother accepted the LORD as her personal Savior. She told me so. She is in Heaven, and I will see her again because Jesus told her so. Even though my mother did not get baptized, she still entered into Heaven. You see, baptism is not a requirement that must be met before you can enter into Heaven. However, it is very important as it is the first step of obedience to God and an outward expression or symbol of Jesus' death, burial and resurrection.

Salvation is the acceptance of Jesus Christ as being the full payment of our sins, not plus or minus anything else. There were two malefactors with Jesus the day of His death. One was on His right side and the other on His left; they were also to be put to death. *Luke 23:39-43* says, *"And one of the malefactors which were hanged railed on him, saying, If thou be Christ, save thyself and us. But the other answering rebuked him, saying, Dost not thou fear God, seeing thou art in the same condemnation? And we indeed justly; for we receive the due reward of our deeds: but this man hath done nothing amiss. And he said unto Jesus, Lord, remember me when thou comest into thy kingdom.*

And Jesus said unto him, Verily I say unto thee, Today shalt thou be with me in paradise."

The malefactor could not get down off the Cross and get baptized before he was put to death, but Jesus said he would be with him in paradise that very day. My mother could not get off her deathbed either. That is the reason for believing that Christ's death paid it all. Nothing else is needed, or it would keep those who could not make it to the baptismal waters from getting into Heaven. Now if you are able to get baptized, you should. Remember, it is the first step of obedience to God.

On October 1, 1989, I accepted the Lord as my personal Savior. Someone had forgotten to plug in the baptismal tub, and those waters were very cold. The pastor of the church told me if I wanted to wait until the following Sunday to get baptized, I could. I said, "NO, if Christ was willing to walk to the Cross for me, I am willing be baptized in cold water for Him."

I was also very delighted to know that I could not lose my place in Heaven. Once saved by grace, always saved by grace. That is called the security of the believer. Notice the words of Jesus as they are in the King James Version, ***John 10:28-30: "And I give unto them eternal life; and they shall never perish, neither shall any man pluck them out of my hand. My Father, which gave them me, is greater than all; and no man is able to pluck them out of my Father's hand. I and my Father are one."***

In fact, you cannot jump out of His hand either, no more than you could tell your mother she did not give birth to you and it be true. A birth is a birth and cannot be reversed! The only difference in the spiritual birth is, it must come from your heart. You have to really believe that you are a sinner, have sinned against God, and accept Jesus' death as full payment for all of your sins—past, present and future.

Resting in that assurance, I began a new life. My walk has included Jesus from that very day. He will continue to teach me all I need to know if I let Him. All I have to do is ask.

I had lots of questions. He answered them and has many more since that time. I still have questions; He still has the answers. I finally put down my life's map. I traded it in for a better one, God's already written, never-changing WORD.

The Bible, as I would soon discover, was the only map I would need. It, to my surprise, was the manual I needed to raise my children. I've no doubt that it would have been the saving grace of my marriage, too. I believe it is the only manual I will ever need for everyday life. It is also the best map.

I smile every time I get lost now, cannot find the right street, or take a wrong turn on one of the many freeways; I have ended up in lots of cities I have never even heard of before. Now, I just enjoy the scenery, lost for the moment, but on my way to Heaven forever. I do delight in the fact I now drive God's car, for which He provides the gas, and He is in control at all times.

Oh, how I thank God for the opportunity for a "whosoever" like me to have a choice in spending eternity with Him in Heaven. Just think, I was headed for an eternity in Hell, with no hope of ever leaving the everlasting flames of fire Satan had in store for me. Because no one knows the day he will die, I think **2 Corinthians 6:2** says it all, *"...behold, now is the accepted time; behold, now is the day of salvation."* The Bible also says in **Matthew 7:7, 8,** *"Ask, and it shall be given you; seek, and ye shall find; knock, and it shall be opened unto you: For every one that asketh receiveth; and he that seeketh findeth; and to him that knocketh it shall be opened."*

I pray, if a "whosoever" is reading this now who has not accepted Jesus Christ from your heart as your personal

Savior, you might do so today, for we know not the hour we will slip away. I pray that you will not let pride keep you from spending an eternity with God, the Creator of your life. I pray also that you have not let false preaching or teaching confuse you and that you know, for sure, you are on your way to Heaven.

I knew a woman who thought she was saved. For years she told everyone that she was a Christian. But she never had any peace. I started going to the same church she went to, and I got saved. I found peace and grew in the Lord, but she was always fretting and angry. I knew she was mad at God too because her youngest son had died. The son was just eighteen years old, and she blamed God for her loss. She went to his graveside every day that she could.

For almost seventeen years, her focus was only on her dead son, and she grew more bitter every day. Before she died though, the day came when she realized she was not really saved after all. She had been under false preaching and teaching as a teenager and was led to believe that all she had to do was repeat a prayer and off to Heaven she would go.

I often wondered why she was always trying to work things out herself and was frustrated because she couldn't, why she acted one way in church, but once she got home, you had a hard time believing she was the same person. It seemed strange to me because at the church we attended, the plan of salvation was preached right out of the King James Bible.

Then one day the doctor told her she had cancer. She was then living in another state, but I saw her often. She was attending a certain type of church and loving every minute of it. The next time I saw her she was attending yet another type of church and loving every minute of that. But through God's Word, she had come to the realization she was not saved after all.

She was in town again when she told me her new testimony and asked me what she should do. I told her to go back to the church we had attended and tell the preacher all about it because all those people had heard her say she was saved.

She did go to the preacher, and he told her she needed to stand before the church congregation and tell them her testimony. Now I know that sounds a bit harsh, but there was a very good reason for having her to do that.

First, was she willing to set her pride aside and let everyone know she had just now accepted the Lord? (If I, as a new believer, could see her lack of faith and trust in the Lord, others could see it.) Second, if there was anyone else in the congregation who had been under false teaching or without full understanding, this would give him or her the courage to come forth, too.

Well, that is exactly what happened. Two other women in the church came forth, realizing they too needed to accept the Lord from their hearts. Just repeating a prayer after someone is not salvation. Both had proclaimed salvation and even been baptized, but were not saved.

False teaching can take you to Hell. When a person is saved, no matter what day that is, he should never be ashamed to let others know what Christ did for him. Who knows? It may even allow someone else to see his need for salvation, too. I am glad I am saved! I am glad that I know it for sure! I am glad she finally knew it for sure, too. There was a change in her. With no more struggle, she went Home to be with the Lord in peace.

If you do not make a conscious decision to accept the LORD as your personal Savior, if you think another day would be a better day, or if you think you need more time to think about it, you have actually chosen Satan instead. *John 3:3* says, *"Verily, verily, I say unto thee, Except a man be born again, he cannot see the kingdom of God."*

Well, it does not end there either...

Chapter 4

I Promise You, Lord

I must tell you, after I got saved, I did not change right away. I pretty much continued on in the same lifestyle as before my salvation. However, God was showing me things daily. I think the first thing I realized was… life is not all about me!

I was very excited about being a Christian. I wanted to do all kinds of things to serve the Lord, and God wanted me to do them, too. I had to start somewhere, but where? By now my ex-husband's son and I were attending church every time the doors were open. We wanted to share our newfound joy with others. We invited everyone we knew to come to church with us, including my ex-husband and our youngest son. Well, of course they wanted nothing to do with that. But we just kept asking them anyway. And they just kept saying, "No, thank you anyway."

I understood. Not so long ago I had been saying the same thing myself. I prayed, "Use me," and God took me up on it. I prayed, "Make me what I ought to be to glorify You, Lord."

Now in order for me to be able to glorify God, I needed to have faith and trust in Him fully because, according to

Hebrews 11:6, "... without faith it is impossible to please him: for he that cometh to God must believe that he is, and that he is a rewarder of them that diligently seek him." I was doing okay so far. I had accepted the Lord as my personal Savior. There's the faith. I got baptized—in that breathtakingly cold water! That was the first step of obedience and identifying myself with Christ's death, burial and resurrection.

My new birth's being announced, I was willing to serve the Lord in any way. I prayed, "Use me, Lord" every day. Little by little He began to prompt me in the areas of my life that needed changing, this, of course, being for my own good.

Some things were not a problem, but some were! I had smoked for eighteen years and had tried to quit many times with no success. Now I want you to know, those cigarettes did not have a mouth, but they told me what to do and when to do it. That "idol" had control over me, and it was very powerful. I know because I could run out of anything in the cupboards and would add it to a list, but if it was cigarettes, I went to the store right then—not for just one pack, either. It would be one or two cartons because, at two or three packs a day, they went fast.

It was annoying, not only to those I smoked around, but to me. I noticed what an inconvenience smoking had become, and that annoyed me, too. They really had a powerful hold on me. I went out in all kinds of weather, night or day, sick or not. There was just nothing convenient about smoking, not to mention what a mess cigarettes were or that my car and house smelled of nastiness. So, I spent a lot of time cleaning because of them, too.

This is how I gave them up in one day: I promised God I would never smoke another cigarette again as long as I walked the face of this earth if He would take the desire for smoking away from me and replace it with a desire to serve Him more.

I told my family of the promise, and none of them believed me! The nerve! Well, the cigarettes had made a liar of me many times before, so I couldn't blame them for not believing me this time either. Only time would prove I meant it, and God would receive all the glory for it.

I did okay for a few days, and then I ran across an opened pack of cigarettes while cleaning. Actually, there were cigarettes everywhere, but this time I weakened. With the garage key and lighter in one hand and a cigarette in the other, out I went. Every step of the way, I thought to myself, "No one will know; the garage is big and airy; the smell will go away before anyone comes home. Nobody will ever find out." With the key just about in the lock, I stopped. "Nobody will know but…God!" He sees all, knows all, hears all, and is in control of all. And I then remembered the promise I had made to Him, the One Who could take the last breath that I needed to walk the face of this earth. There I was, about to break a promise to the One Who never breaks a promise, to the One Whose Son willingly died for me so I could spend eternity in Heaven with Him.

How ungrateful and selfish could I possibly be? I asked God again right then and there to take that desire from me. Again I asked Him to give me a stronger desire to serve Him. As I slithered back into the house, I thanked God for His grace and mercy and for the strength He had given me to get me through that time of weakness. That bondage had been broken. I can still say, and only by the grace of God can I say it, the promise was not broken, and I was not found to be a liar this time. For over eighteen years, God has kept that desire from me, and I still have a desire to serve Him more.

With that out of the way, I was faced with the next nagging thing I couldn't eliminate. I was living in the same house with my ex-husband. I did not come from a divorced family, but I had experienced two in my life already. *Mark 10:3-9* says, *"And he answered and said unto them, What did Moses command you? And they said, Moses suffered to write a bill of divorcement, and to put her away. And Jesus answered and said unto them, For the hardness of your heart he wrote you this precept. But from the beginning of the creation God made them male and female. For this cause shall a man leave his father and mother, and cleave to his wife; And they twain shall be one flesh: so then they are no more twain, but one flesh. What therefore God hath joined together, let not man put asunder."*

This even means the two people who married each other. I, for one, was totally devastated. I did see some of the effects it had on our three little boys, most irreversible. Now, many years later, remarriage had been mentioned several times, and I had no desire to jump back into that fire. Pressure was applied in many areas of my life, and I called on the Lord for direction. I was under conviction but did not recognize it as the Lord dealing with me. I just saw it as a very lousy and uncomfortable feeling. I listened intently and wanted the Lord to tell me what to do next.

At this point in my life, working at a worldwide corporation and putting in unbelievable hours, I was so busy that I met myself coming and going most days. I had managed not to miss an opportunity to attend church though. My ex-husband talked about us getting married again. That thought had occurred to me also, and we had even talked about it, but...boy, oh, boy. I could almost see how that would go, not seeing any changes in him. Why would I want to do that? We could not agree on very many things as it was. Now I was saved, and he wasn't.

I felt very uneasy about it. I knew about *2 Corinthians 6:14: "Be ye not unequally yoked together with unbelievers: for what fellowship hath righteousness with unrighteousness? and what communion hath light with darkness?"* So, maybe not! More time went by, and soon the ex-husband was attending church with us more and more. Our youngest son, who had accepted the Lord as his personal Savior at the age of ten, had decided to rededicate his life to the Lord and attended church on a regular basis, too.

February 1990 was not to be forgotten. Again the pressure was on in so many areas of my life. The marriage issue was the biggest burden. I simply did not want to look another failed marriage in the eye. Life goes on, and each day gets worse. My work was nearing the busiest time of the year. Five nights of revival meetings were going on at church again, and I did not want to miss a single one of them.

It was cold the morning of February 13, 1990. As I drove to work on the freeway, the windows were up, and I was praying to God. I needed some answers. "Lord, if You want me to marry him, I promise You I will, exactly one year from the day he gets saved. I know, Lord, You don't want me to marry anyone unsaved." I was driving at least 65 miles an hour with only God and me in the car when I made that promise. No chance anyone could have overheard that!

On February 15, 1990, I came home from work, and my ex-husband's son said, "So, Ma, do you want to hear some good news!?"

"Oh, hallelujah, yes, of course I could use some good news. What might that be?" He could hardly contain himself as he let it be known his father had just gotten saved earlier that day.

Well, I bet I don't have to tell you what was running through my mind when I got that fabulous bit of information! Lots of thoughts sprang loose, among them the sound of wedding bells. On one hand I was very excited to know he was on his way to Heaven, but then I remembered the promise to God. Oh, boy! I'm in trouble now!

I knew I was not going to break any promise I had made to God, and I also knew I wasn't going to be able to get through this on my own either. This could only be of the Lord, so I called upon Him right away. "Lord, please help me! Show me what I need to do to glorify You." Leaving my ex-husband completely out of this, I asked God to show ME what I needed to do. I was going to need this information soon as I only had a year!

Remembering how He gave me strength during my last weakness (smoking), I hoped He would do it again. He said He would never leave me nor forsake me, so I claimed that out loud. I couldn't see Him, but I knew He was there.

I can tell you that God went right to work. There was no delay in some of the answers He had in store for me. The pruning had begun! Reading my Bible daily, I could see all kinds of things that were in my life that shouldn't be and lots that should've been, but weren't. God revealed things to me daily, and I couldn't believe I had been wrong again.

In many ways, life was about me! I wasn't perfect, and I knew that. The biggest surprise was that I wasn't even good. ***Romans 3:12* says, *"They are all gone out of the way, they are together become unprofitable; there is none that doeth good, no, not one." Romans 3:23* adds, *"For all have sinned, and come short of the glory of God."*** I had fallen short, and by God's grace, He had forgiven me. He was then and is now still willing to show me the way. I hated looking at all the wreck and ruin in my life—mostly, the end result of my disobedience and selfishness. Then there was the anger and bitterness with some revenge crowding in, followed by disappointment and a huge broken heart.

Now seeing the truth, how on earth was I going to get through it? I was looking at the consequences of choices I had made over the years: responding out of anger and frustration, not looking past the moment, running away, looking for that ideal life I had imagined. The consequences had not just affected me though. The ripple effect is deep and wide and should be looked at before making any decision.

I knew I was going to have to start living in such a manner that would be glorifying to God. Here I was, living in the same house as my ex-husband and going to church, acting as if not a single thing was wrong. However, I was feeling the weight of God's conviction. Hypocrisy! What could be worse?

I wanted to tell my ex-husband of the promise I had made to God so he would, hopefully, lighten up on what had become constant nagging about getting remarried. I attempted to tell him twice, although neither time went very well. On the first attempt, we were driving down the street. I was about to give him all the details of the promise when a car pulled out in front of us. It came so close to causing what could have been a very bad accident that our minds were on that the rest of the way home. On the second attempt, we had been having a lovely conversation, and I thought this would be the perfect time to mention "the promise." But the biggest argument broke out, and to this day, I still do not know what triggered it. Needless to say, I did not breathe a single word about it that day either.

God had intervened both times. I didn't recognize it as that at first, but on the third attempt, I just stopped, sensing it would be better to wait. I was convinced God wanted that promise between just Him and me for the time being. It was as though He said, "This is not yours to tell, so just wait on Me."

I waited on Him, but I waited at my youngest sister's house. I moved in with her until February 15, 1991, the day my first ex-husband became my husband again. In that waiting period, God showed me more and more of what needed changing in my life.

Psalms 51:17: "The sacrifices of God are a broken spirit: a broken and a contrite heart, O God, thou wilt not despise." This time I found myself standing in the office of the justice of the peace without my mother or father at my side as I said, "I do." Instead, our two oldest sons, two granddaughters, and a daughter-in-law witnessed that union.

My husband's son went to live with his mother on June 10, 1991, a very sad day for us. This is evidence of what divorce can do to the people we love. With his father and me married, his hopes and dreams of that perfect life he had imagined were gone, too. Children hold out a hope that their parents will somehow get back together. They blame themselves, wondering if they caused the problem. They can't put it in proper perspective because the ones who caused it are the selfish adults. I am convinced the Bible would have been the saving grace of my marriage.

Chapter 5

The Pruning of My Orchard

I retired on February 11, 1991. Yes, I checked with the Lord first. I took that step of faith. It meant half of our income, and things did get very interesting. I had no idea what the Lord had in store for me, but I took the "step" anyway.

We had a pretty fabulous nest egg gathering interest daily, so "not to worry." I should have suspected something was up; nest egg and faith are not compatible. *Hebrews 11:1* says, *"Now faith is the substance of things hoped for, the evidence of things not seen."*

Right about this time, I learned the meaning of a lot of words located in the Bible. Faith was about to show me its true meaning and how it really worked. Our nest egg was visible, but not for long; February 12, 1991, I did not have to go to work. Oh, what a glorious day. We bought a new car February 28 and paid cash for it. Oh, what a glorious day. On March 4, the bank called the mortgage loan on my mother-in-law's house. My husband and I had promised to take care of that for her. Oh, what an eye opening day!

We had more than enough money to pay the loan…by three dollars. This meant I would have to wait a few more days until my husband got paid for money to go to Arizona to sign the final papers and hand over the balance of our nest egg.

One benefit of my retiring was this would be the first year I would be able to attend the women's retreat from beginning to end. I could hardly wait! Oh, what a glorious few days that would be. There was going to be a speaker on "The Virtuous Woman." Great, I wanted to meet her. Not knowing all there was to know about the "The Virtuous Woman," I asked God to show me. Well, can I let you in on some inside information? Don't ask Him unless you really want to know! Oh, what an eye-opening day that turned out to be!

I remember I couldn't wait for the retreat to get over. I was under such conviction, I just wanted to disappear. To my knowledge, that wasn't likely to happen unless death occurred. My suspicions had been confirmed though. I was not "The Virtuous Woman." With this information, I asked the Lord to show me what I would have to do to become one. Oh, what a painful day.

It was even more painful when I made the declaration to my husband that I had no virtues. He, being kind, said, "Oh, yes, you do." I wanted to know which one that might be. He said, "Name them."

So I quickly turned to Proverbs 31, named a few, and said, "Well?"

His reply, "Keep reading."

I named a few more and said, "Well?"

Again, his reply was, "Keep reading." I named a few more and just looked at him. He said, "Keep reading." That is when I told him there were no more to read.

Quickly, he said, "Read them to me again. There must be at least one." Well, I didn't want him feeling forced to lie to me just to make me feel better! I'd rather have the horrifying news all at once. The fact was I had no virtues at all…

With my asking, God took out His pruning shears and began His work. My suspicions confirmed once again, yes,

My Father In Heaven My Father On Earth

this was going to take a lifetime. Oh, what a painful yet glorious time. My Father in Heaven cared for me, while lovingly trimming away things that must be removed to make way for new growth.

Isn't it funny how we pray, our prayer is answered, and we do not recognize it as answered prayer? That is because it wasn't answered in the way we imagined it would be or by the time we wanted it to be. My prayer was that God would show me some things. I wanted to know more about "The Virtuous Woman." I wanted to be more like her. "Make me what I ought to be, Lord." I just wanted to be a glory to God.

I was willing to serve the Lord in any way. I prayed, "Use me, Lord," every day. Little by little, He began to do just that.

I was asked to be a nursery worker (prayer answered, but not the way I expected). I had no desire to be in the nursery. My children were all well past that stage, and I came to church to hear the Word of God, not to be the babysitter. However, when explained to me how the parents of those children needed to hear the Word of God in order to know better how to raise them, I saw the need and accepted that challenge.

I was asked to teach Sunday school. Again a prayer was answered, but absolutely not the way I had expected. I wanted to serve the Lord, yes, but teaching! Yikes! OH, FABULOUS! How was I going to tell the preacher I couldn't do that? His children were in that class, and they would surely know more about the Sunday school lessons than I did. Then it came to mind: I had said I was willing to serve in any way. I had not added, "except for that, Lord." So, I accepted that challenge too, which made me read my Bible more, and I studied as I had never studied before. I still prayed, "Use me, Lord." Only this time I asked Him for more, I added;

"make me what I ought to be to glorify You Lord, and give me wisdom, grace and understanding."

In June of 1991, I started a small craft business out of my home. Not working now, there was lots of time for shopping, gardening, sewing, and even a cake decorating class. This was a resting time for me, doing the fun things I had always wanted to do, but for which I had never had time. God was still in charge of my life.

I noticed I was managing my time better. Making quilts and dolls for my customers meant I had to work diligently, be organized, and plan ahead. Our youngest son was in college and working. With his living in the mother-in-law's quarters right out our back door, the "empty nest syndrome" had begun but was not yet in full effect. All was well. We were still in an adjusting and resting period, but God's pruning was taking place. I could see it, and I could feel it.

In 1986, my father retired, sold his house in Arizona, and moved to California. On Easter Sunday 1991, my father accepted the Lord as his personal Savior, and his life began to change. Even this was out of character for him. He had claimed to be an atheist all his life and said he didn't believe there was a God at all. But I, for one, had been praying God would show him his need for Christ.

It was right around that time that my father started coming down more often to go to church with us. He didn't come down every Sunday, or on a regular basis, just more often. He would tell us some really unbelievable things, but he still seemed like he knew what he was talking about. Something just didn't seem right, but I could never figure out what that something was.

Even though he was only an hour and a half's drive away from us, I called him often. He lived alone, and there were times I wondered and worried about him. He would tell me about things he had done, and I could hardly believe what he was telling me—some outrageous thing that seemed impossible for his age and health condition. There were times he would not sound like himself, or his speech would be so slurred, I thought he might have been drinking. He was a drinker in times past, but as far as I knew, he only had an occasional drink, and certainly not at the early hour I called.

In January of 1994, a dear friend of my fathers was dying of cancer, and my father wanted to go see him before that happened. My sister and her husband were hoping to get to see the friend, too. When she mentioned this to our father, he assumed they would be coming by to pick him up and that he would be riding with them. She tried to clarify that they were only hoping to get to go but were not yet sure. Her husband would need to apply for vacation because of the traveling distance. They lived in Arizona, my father lived in California, and the friend, because of his illness, was in Seattle, Washington.

My father could only ask the same question, "What time will you be by to pick me up?" No matter what she said, his only reply was, "What time will you be by to pick me up?" This was not only odd, but also very frustrating to her. However, they did make the arrangements and did go by and pick him up. The two-day trip was, I am sure, a memorable one. They said he talked endlessly. Once they arrived, he visited with his friend a few hours and was ready to go home.

My sister thought they would stop by and visit my father's half-brother, but my father showed no interest in that at all. He just wanted to go home. She again tried to explain that the trip was tiring and they would need rest before going home. He wasn't concerned with that information either; he just wanted to go home. In their opinion, he was being quite selfish when he made it sound as though it were a 20-mile drive and there should be no need for rest.

His friend died a week later, and my father seemed distant in that knowledge. He was affected by it, but did not have the reaction I thought he would. It was like it was only a name to him, not a person he had known for over fifty years, like it did not register completely. He had a vague look on his face, like complete acceptance, but without emotions of any kind. It was that type of strangeness that happened among perfectly normal things that made it all very difficult to detect a problem.

None of us spent hour after hour or even day after day with him to see how often this strange behavior took place. We overlooked a lot of it, blaming it on his becoming more selfish as he got older. Living alone, maybe falling into a rut, and not having to consider anyone but himself on a daily basis.

In September of 1994, my father called me and asked if he could park his car in our driveway for a few months. He was going to take a train trip to Iowa and help the wife of his friend who had died in January. Now that her husband was gone, she wanted to move to Donna, Texas, to be closer to her family. He wanted to know if I would take him to the train depot. He planned to stay until after Thanksgiving, but to spend Christmas with us and would be returning by plane. He wanted to know if I could I possibly pick him up at the airport at that time?

Of course, all the answers were "Yes." But I was concerned. The reason he was taking the trip was to do the driving of this lady's motor home. From Iowa to Texas was a distance of hundreds of miles, and they would be towing a car! His driving skills had diminished considerably, and he had rolled his own motor home in 1986 while towing a vehicle! I shouldn't have worried. Those concerns were nothing compared to what really took place.

He assured me he had enough medication to last while he was away from his doctors. He seemed a bit nervous, and I passed it off as excitement and anticipation of the long train ride. Waving good-bye, not expecting to see him for a few months, I went home feeling very uneasy about the whole thing.

He was gone about ten days when the phone call came. It was the friend's wife, saying she had put my father on a bus headed for Arizona early that morning. My sister and her husband would be going to the bus station at 11:30 a.m. the next day to visit with him while he waited out a four-hour layover at the Phoenix bus station. I would need to pick him up 8:30 that same evening when he arrived at the San Bernardino bus station. Oh, boy, what was this all about?

However, this was not the most alarming news I would receive. The next call came from my sister. She was relaying a message: our father had called just as they were walking out the door to go meet him at the bus station. They would not have to come to the bus station after all. The bus driver was holding up the bus so Dad could make the call to her. He told her he would be in California in four hours and for her to call me and have me pick him up at the bus station at 4 p.m.

This did not sound right at all. Things were not adding up. First of all, bus drivers do not hold up the bus schedule for anyone to make a phone call. Second, unless you are on a plane, it takes longer than four hours to travel from Phoenix, Arizona, to San Bernardino, California, even on a non-stop express bus. I thought maybe she had misunderstood him, so I repeated what she had said to verify my understanding. I understood what she had said, but I did not understand what was going on.

I called the friend, now in Donna, Texas. The itinerary was close, but the times were way off. She said, "It was pretty strange. Just out of nowhere, he wanted to go home, and he was going that day." There was no talking him out of it. With no flights going out when he wanted to leave, she made arrangements and took him to the bus station. At the end of our conversation, she asked me to call her upon his arrival.

My husband and I went to the bus station and waited. The bus arrived, but my father was not on it. This really didn't surprise me. I knew if he was in Phoenix when he called, as he said he was, he couldn't have been on that bus.

We checked to see when the next bus was scheduled to arrive. Great, now we would have to miss church because it wasn't due until 8 p.m. The 8:00 bus arrived, but my father was not on it either! Now what? We checked the time for the next bus coming in. Midnight! Fabulous, we would get to come back yet one more time that night. Isn't that special? At this point, I was more scared than irritated, but irritation wasn't very far away.

We went home, and I called my sister in Arizona to see if she had heard from our father. No, she hadn't, so we went over the previous phone call from our father one more time. Nothing had changed; all I could do now was wait. Nothing had changed at the bus station either, except this time the bus was late. When the bus finally arrived, my husband actually got on the bus to make sure my father hadn't fallen asleep. No, he was not on the bus, sleeping or otherwise, and there would be no more buses until 8:00 the next morning! What were we going to do? Pray to God, that's what!

Where do you start looking for an adult who should have been home, according to him, eight hours ago? I started making phone calls, one right after another, rehashing every conversation just to make sure I hadn't missed a clue of some sort. I called the bus station in Los Angeles, thinking perhaps he might have fallen asleep on an earlier bus and ended up there. The station was already closed, and the janitor said the place was empty.

At 1:00 a.m. I called the police. A very nice lady officer arrived at 1:30. She was very compassionate as she explained that a missing persons report could not be filed until he had been missing at least 24 hours! And to make matters even more complicated, it could only be filed by the last person to see him. So the plot thickened, moment by moment. Who was the last person to see him? The lady who lived in Donna, Texas! I could not sleep. All sorts of thoughts came up for consideration, all of them too scary to keep thinking about. Where could he possibly be?

With the time difference, I didn't think 4:00 a.m. California time would be too soon to call Texas. I wanted that report filed as soon as possible. She took down all the instructions needed and said she would get back with me as soon as it was completed.

I still had my craft business that had an 800 number for phone orders. I had given my father one of my business cards, and the 800 number was on the card.

The next disturbing phone call came at 8:00 the next morning. The man on the other end of the phone said he was a security guard at the Radisson Hotel, stated my father's name, and asked me if I knew him. I said I did, and the guard handed the phone to my father. My father asked me if I could come pick him up. Of course I said yes and asked him where he was. The security guard got back on the phone to give me directions. He said my father would be waiting at the parking lot entrance gate of the Radisson Hotel in San Bernardino. About what time would I be picking him up? To be on the safe side, I said in about 30 minutes. The man thanked me and said he would be waiting.

My husband had already gone to work, but our youngest son was still home. I asked him if he would go with me to pick up Grandpa. No one but the LORD will ever know how grateful I was when he said, "Yes."

I was not prepared for what I saw or heard. My father spotted my car before I ever spotted him. He came, almost running toward us, before I had a chance to even pull to the curb. He looked as if he had been working on the bus for days, not riding it! He was greasy and filthy, from head to toe. Well, I was shocked at the sight of him, but even more so as I listened to the security guard tell me the events that had led up to the phone call I had received that morning.

The guard had found him huddled in some bushes, scared half out of his mind. My father told him that he had been drugged and needed to talk to the FBI as soon as possible, that he had valuable information that must be imparted before he was killed. People were after him, and he had to get home right away, and could he please make a phone call to his daughter at this number? She will know what to do. (Well, she didn't know what to do! And once she knew what needed to be done, she didn't want to do it!)

My father got in the car and talked to me as normal as normal could be. Then he noticed my son in the back seat and asked who he was. When I told him it was his grandson, he was shocked. He didn't know he even had a grandson. Fear increased as I began to ask him questions. "Dad, where are your glasses?"

His reply was, "They got knocked off during the fight."

So, I asked him, "What fight are you talking about, and who were you fighting with?"

He said, "The bus driver."

I could not believe what I was hearing, "Dad, you had a fight with the bus driver? Why?"

"Because he wouldn't let me off the bus when I wanted to get off."

"So, Dad, where are we supposed to pick up your luggage?"

He nonchalantly said, "I don't know. It was still on the bus when I got kicked off for fighting."

My head was spinning so fast by now, I even hated to ask where he got kicked off the bus, but I went for it anyway. He didn't know, but he thought it was by the train station. Fabulous! I can only guess that he was on the 8:00 p.m. bus the day before and didn't know where his stop was. He probably recognized the train depot he had left thirteen days earlier and thought that was where he was supposed to get off. When the bus driver refused to let him off, the fight began.

Oh, dear Heavenly Father! What to do next? We drove home. Dad had no luggage, no glasses, and no medicine. I had a feeling he had not eaten or had his medicine for a long while, most likely the whole trip back. He didn't want to take a shower or go to the doctor, and he needed both desperately. I knew he loved the pastor of our church, so I called him. The pastor, being a very kind man, came right away. He was able to talk my father into letting me take him to the veterans' hospital for a check-up. I made a quick call to Texas to let our friend know we had found my father. I also asked her if she would cancel the missing persons report and said I would call her later to let her know how things turned out.

If I remember correctly, the word "dementia" immediately put me on the edge of my seat. The doctor examined my father physically and tested him mentally. Though the doctor was uncertain what was really going on with my father's health right at that moment, he did know he should not live alone anymore. He would need a caregiver!!!

All kinds of frightening thoughts flew through my head. I believe "panic" would be a good word to use. WOW! I couldn't even think clearly. I tried to figure out what to do next, but I couldn't think at all! What could this possibly mean? The first thing I needed to do was to go home. Yes, that's what I would do. I'd go home. I would talk this over with my husband and my three sisters. Certainly they would have some answers to this frightening situation.

I have had some very difficult and challenging things happen in my life, but nothing like this life changer. Alzheimer's disease was brought up later on. And I cannot tell you how grateful I am those were not the first words I had to digest. "Dementia" and "caregiver" in the same sentence were breathtaking enough. I didn't know my Father in Heaven had already begun preparing me for the task of caring for my father on earth.

Chapter 6

Thanks, Lord, But No Thanks

So...I was elected to be the caregiver of my father. One sister lived in Arizona, another lived in Georgia, and the third lived near me in California, but worked eight hours a day.

I asked my husband what we were going to do. By now it was just he and I living in the house, and we had a spare bedroom. "There is no one to take care of my father but us. Do you mind? Would it be okay to have my father move in and live with us for who knows how long?"

His answer was, "Yes, it will be okay."

This meant so many things would be changing. I would soon have to give up my little business just to keep up with the demands that were placed on me. And though I had taken him at his word and didn't realize it at the time, my husband didn't really mean it when he said it would be okay for my father to move in.

As I was saying, God was very busy with me. In order to glorify the Lord, I would have to have faith and trust in Him fully. I was not at that point yet. Faith. Yes, I had faith. Obviously, only as small as a grain of a mustard seed though, because I was trying to figure out how this was going to work out. There was no need for me to put myself through all that. My Father in Heaven already knew just what I was to do. He sent me bulletins right out of the Bible. **Hebrews 13:5** says, *"Let your conversation be without covetousness; and be content with such things as ye have: for he hath said, I will never leave thee, nor forsake thee."*

Well, my conversation, the way I acted or reacted to this new situation in my life, was not good. I was coveting my life the way it used to be—in other words, acting nothing like Christ. So I did the only thing I knew to do in such a predicament—I got busy, busy sending out invitations to my pity party.

Have you ever noticed the only people who show up to your pity party are the ones who want more pity from you than they are willing to give you? Well, there is one exception to that rule. If you are one of Gods children, just look around. The Lord will be there with a lot to offer. It's just not going to be pity.

I had the privilege of caring for my father for six and one-half years. Now I didn't pray, "Dear Heavenly Father, please let me put my life on hold so I can take care of my father here on earth." No, remember I prayed, "Use me, Lord." And God took me up on it. I prayed, "Make me what I ought to be to glorify you, Lord." Let me start off by telling you, I didn't see it as a privilege at first. The fact was, I saw it as the biggest challenge ever. And it didn't end there either.

When you are heavily burdened with the cares of this world, when you think you cannot do one…more…thing…, yet that one…more…thing…comes along anyway, don't forget to call upon the Lord. We have a tendency to wonder where God is during these times. Well, at least I did then, and still do from time to time. I have to remind myself that God knows all, sees all, and hears all. He even knows what is coming next and just how I am going to react to it. I am always amazed at how God has never given up on me.

There are so many promises of God that I can't name them all. Some I call upon daily. There is one that is such a wonderful encouragement to me. Let me share it with you. ***Matthew 11:28* says, *"Come unto me, all ye that labour and are heavy laden and I will give you rest."***

With hindsight in my favor, I see just what a privilege caring for my father really was. It was probably the most difficult thing I have ever had to do. It is never easy to watch one of your parents fall into the grips of a mental infirmity, no matter what the disease is called.

Dementia is not a disease, just a group of symptoms. The symptoms are the clues doctors use to determine the disease. The most common cause of dementia is Alzheimer's. That is a very hard diagnosis for doctors to make because Alzheimer's disease is confirmed by an autopsy.

There were many tests my father went through that led the doctors to their diagnosis. He had many other health issues besides the loss of memory and behavioral problems. He suffered mini strokes in the brain, seizures from a severe head injury, type II diabetes, and nutritional deficiencies. He had already had one heart attack, so the hypertension and high cholesterol could cause another one at any time without warning. There are so many stages everyone has to go through—the person with the disease and those caring for him. The memory loss was very difficult for my father. That, of course, was the reason he needed a caregiver.

My husband told me that one day he and my father were in the garage and my father said, "Sometimes I don't know what I am saying or what I am doing, so will you stop me when you see me like that?" So he knew there was something wrong; he just couldn't tell anyone what that something was. The most difficult part for me was to have to watch it happen and to know how to handle each situation. There were many of those situations too, one right after another.

Let me see...caregiver, custodian, overseer, watchman, guardian, and nutritionist. Are you kidding me? This was going to be a very time-consuming, life-altering task, one that couldn't be done properly unless I had the right heart. I knew I did not have the right heart. How dare everyone just expect me to put my life aside while they continue on with theirs as if nothing had changed!

The Lord had been answering my prayers, just not in the manner I expected. I was looking for an immediate solution to the situation, but God had something else in mind. He started with pointing out my selfishness. WOW, that was painful, but so needed, once I saw how horrible it looked to the saved and unsaved. I had to give more than just time to this crisis; it took planning work and patience. Before selfishness was finished, God grabbed a hand full of bad attitude. God's working in my life was a challenge, because Satan had ruled in that area of my life for a very long time. We all know, "Old habits are hard to break."

Another bulletin began to flash before my eyes. *Ephesians 6:10-12* says, *"Finally, my brethren, be strong in the Lord, and in the power of his might. Put on the whole armour of God, that ye may be able to stand against the wiles of the devil. For we wrestle not against flesh and blood, but against principalities, against powers, against the rulers of the darkness of this world, against spiritual wickedness in high places."*

Resentment had raised its ugly head, and bitterness wasn't far behind. Good thing I had accepted the Sunday school teaching offer that caused me to study so hard. *Second Timothy 2:15* says, *"Study to show thyself approved unto God, a workman that needeth not to be ashamed, rightly dividing the word of truth."* The book of Proverbs was another lifesaver for me. *Proverbs 3:5-6* says, *"Trust in the LORD with all thine heart; and lean not unto thine own understanding. In all thy ways acknowledge him, and he shall direct thy paths."* It didn't stop there, either. Verses 7 and 8 say, *"Be not wise in thine own eyes: fear the LORD, and depart from evil. It shall be health to thy navel, and marrow to thy bones."* I did need that information, and I fell back on it often.

As I mentioned, my father on earth had accepted the Lord as his personal Savior a few years before his diagnosis, so he and I would read the Bible together every morning. Those are precious memories for sure. Alzheimer's disease has been broken down into several stages. One does not die of Alzheimer's; one dies with it.

He came to us at stage four. The forgetfulness was a bit trying, and the stubbornness was taxing, but the excessive talking was on the last frayed nerve I had. I needed more grace in this area; that was for sure. God was still very busy, working with me and answering my prayers at the same time. I was still teaching Sunday school, working in the nursery, picking people up for church, and going soul winning, plus doing all the things I had to do for my family. I was not complaining at this point, just explaining.

I see how God has answered my prayers regularly, but not as I had envisioned. I think the worst part about the whole thing is, I already knew the Scripture, but was not following it. I had read through the Bible at least eight times. I studied it and taught it. I believed it and thought I was living it. That was until God showed me more of what needed changing in me.

God is a patient and loving God. He just keeps working with you until you get it the way He wants it. *Psalms 103:13-14* says, *"Like as a father pitieth his children, so the LORD pitieth them that fear him. For he knoweth our frame; he remembereth that we are dust."*

Day after day my father got a bit worse, and it was as though I was the only one who noticed. He was right there in front of me and never left that last, very fragile, frayed nerve of mine. Okay, now I was complaining. I was asking for help from anyone, just a little time to myself. There were no takers except for my husband's aunt, the 74-year-old-mother of "the preacher of the family."

My father had to be watched 24 hours a day. Fabulous—and me without sleep or help. I frantically sent out more invitations to my next pity party. No takers that time, either. It was just me and the Lord.

On November 14, 1995, I received a phone call from those fabulous, lifelong friends who had opened up their home to us when we first arrived in Arizona. The wife was in critical condition, and cancer had consumed all but 95 pounds of her. Snow had already started falling for the winter. He would need to leave the hospital every few days to check on their home and the dog in the rural area of Snowflake, Arizona. This was a trip of 85 miles, one way. He would need me to stay at the hospital in Springerville with his wife. The roads were rough, and he could get snowed in. She didn't want to be alone. Could I come right away?

My head was spinning so fast, I could barely think of what to do. I certainly didn't want to let them down in their hour of need. They were like a second set of parents to me and like grandparents to our boys. They had always been there for me, no matter what.

By this time, I had given up my little business. I would only have to make arrangements for the things I was responsible for at the church. I would need to ask my husband if he minded, and I hoped he would agree to let me go because "No" didn't even seem like an option.

My husband said, "Yes, of course. Go." But I would have to take my father with me. Oh, boy, this was going to be a lasting memory, and I was right. It was.

I called the folks back to let them know I would be leaving later that evening. They were aware of my father's condition. I told them he would be coming along, and that was okay with them. I quickly made all the arrangements, packed things for the two of us, and our eleven-hour journey began. That was an experience, to say the least.

It was a very long trip, and I was grateful for his non-stop talking. It kept me awake. We had to stop often to meet his needs, and I was very glad to finally arrive at our destination. However, my father was not ready to retire upon our arrival as I had hoped he would be. I did not know until later, that those with Alzheimer's disease do not do well out of their familiar surroundings. But he was at least cooperative; he just followed me around without complaint, talking every waking moment.

The next day we drove the 85 miles to the hospital in Springerville. Oh, our friend looked so, so bad. She was in good spirits and wanted to talk about the LORD. She gave me her testimony and expressed her concern for her stepson's salvation. I called her son more than once for her and listened as she tried to tell him of the importance of his need for accepting Christ. I still do not know whether or not he ever did accept Christ as his personal Savior.

My father was restless and roamed the halls of this small country hospital of 28 rooms, night and day. The weather was so bitterly cold, and I was getting no sleep. Finally, after a week, I called my husband and asked if he could take some vacation time and let me bring my father home for him to take care of for a while. I knew our friend did not have much more time here on this earth, and there would be things that needed to be taken care of. My husband said he would, and we left very early the next morning.

The trip home was exciting. It started to snow in Flagstaff, Arizona. Great! I had never driven in snow, and I thought, "This could get very interesting." And, I was right! My father's chatter was a comfort to me in one way (it kept my mind very alert), and I listened as he told me how to drive in the snow. Remember, we came from Iowa and he had driven in snow for years. Everything he told me to do was correct, and it worked just the way he said it would as I followed his instructions. I was amazed and skeptical at the same time as he told me what to do just to stay on the road on which I could no longer even see the pavement. He rolled down his window and tried to wipe the snow off the windshield with his hand. He even told me to turn the windshield wipers off so he could wipe the snow off himself. It was a white-knuckle trip, but we avoided joining the multitude of other cars that had landed in the ditch. I will always smile in amazement at how my Father in Heaven helped my father on earth get us through that without incident.

    I started early the next morning for another 14-hour trip. I drove straight to the hospital this time. I prayed for good weather and got it, which was good because I did not have my co-pilot with me this time, and as crazy as it sounds, I missed him. Don't get me wrong: I did enjoy the quiet—I just missed him. I made it back a few days before our friend went home to be with the LORD on Thanksgiving Day. And it was a day of "Thanks giving." I was so thankful that she knew the Lord as her personal Savior.

    After everything was taken care of, I returned home. I noticed a big change for the worse in my father. He was agitated so easily and was always into something. By now, he could not follow simple instructions, and nothing held his attention. But no matter what, he was always willing to read the Bible and go to church. He loved going for rides and wanted to go somewhere every single day. If I was busy or I turned my back for more than a few minutes, off he would go. He would take off, not knowing where he was going, just that he was going.

    I was still praying, "Use me, Lord. Give me wisdom, grace, and understanding. Show me what I need to do to glorify YOU."

"I can't keep up this pace. Lord, where are You? OH, BOY, do I need help! More patience and more faith!" Great, another bulletin: *James 1:2-6* says, *"My brethren, count it all joy when ye fall into divers temptations; Knowing this, that the trying of your faith worketh patience. But let patience have her perfect work, that ye may be perfect and entire, wanting nothing. If any of you lack wisdom, let him ask of God, that giveth to all men liberally, and upbraideth not; and it shall be given him. But let him ask in faith, nothing wavering. For he that wavereth is like a wave of the sea driven with the wind and tossed."*

Fabulous, now I'm wavering. Wouldn't you know it; the more I asked for wisdom, the worse things got. I had my eyes so close to the problem, I could no longer see the Cross. I didn't see God's pruning shears anymore either, but they were there. I knew it because He said He would never leave me nor forsake me, and of course, I felt the pruning big time.

By now, bitterness had me in full bondage. Then, of course, God reminded me of *Hebrews 12:15*: *"Looking diligently lest any man fail of the grace of God; lest any root of bitterness springing up trouble you, and thereby many be defiled."* Spring up? How about tied up and all those watching be defiled. "OH, LORD, where are You? Why are You allowing all this? I don't think I can make it." Just about the time I really wanted to give up, a verse from God's Word would come to mind.

Galatians 6:9 says, *"And let us not be weary in well doing: for in due season we shall reap, if we faint not."* Not only was I weary, but I felt like fainting. But by God's grace, I kept going, and I kept finding more promises to lean upon just to get me through one more day, sometimes one more minute. I tried to keep *Romans 8:28* in mind: *"And we know that all things work together for good to them that love God, to them who are the called according to his pur-*

pose." I did love God, and when I accepted His Son as my personal Savior, I was called according to His purpose. Then I remembered, God had a purpose and a plan for me. I had asked Him to use me, and He did, and even though I didn't know how, He was still using me.

I hope that my trying experiences are not going to a discouragement to anyone. My hope and prayer is that it will be just the opposite—that they will encourage you, not only to look for the promises of God, but to memorize them and call upon them. Use them to get you through those difficult times when you think you might not make it one more second.

I am not going to say any of the trying times were easy or that they got easier as time went on. What I am going to say is, "The LORD GOD HIMSELF walked me through it all, personally." I am better for it, and I thank HIM for it was only through HIS grace that I didn't quit. If getting through trials in life were easy, everyone would be doing it, and where would God get the Glory? Why would we ever need to call upon God at all for anything if we were capable of doing everything on our own? Wouldn't you know it? I had forgotten that very thing as I whimpered and whined about poor me.

I was getting stronger the whole time. I just didn't recognize it because I was so weak, wavering, and ready to faint. God is good. He continued to send me messages right out of His already written Word. Faith, of course, was right behind strength. I knew Satan wanted me to give up, which would ruin my testimony for the Lord and prove that the Lord I was trying to live for was not able to handle my problems. Satan wanted to make it look like the Lord had deserted me when things got difficult. In reality, it would have been my walking away from the Lord when things hadn't gone the way I wanted or expected them to go.

Chapter 7

Is That You, Lord?

All the while I was in the trial of my life, God was still providing so generously. We wanted to buy a house. Fat chance of that though. Remember, I had quit my job—on faith, I might add. The hope of our qualifying for a house was slim to none, as we had found through previous attempts. I prayed God would allow us a home of our own. I prayed specifically, too. "LORD, there is no money for a down payment. It can't cost more than our budget will allow, and if you could make the house payment less than we are paying in rent, that would be so wonderful."

Not to be ungrateful or anything, but I wanted to be sure it was of the Lord. I added, "A big back yard for fruit trees and a garden, a fence for the dogs, but mostly, just let me know it is of You, Lord." I was counting on *Ephesians 3:20: "Now unto him that is able to do exceeding abundantly above all that we ask or think, according to the power that worketh in us."*

My prayer was answered. Every need was met. Why it surprised me, I have no idea, but it did. We found a house, no down payment required. The realtor owned the house, and it was in desperate need of repair, so she offered us a deal we could not refuse. She gave us six months to do those repairs and bring it up to code. When it passed inspection, we would sign the papers, and it would be ours. There was a lot of work involved, but it was worth it. My husband continued at his job while I took care of my father and worked on the house. We hired out all the heavy work I could not do.

In years past, my father had been a handyman. He could do just about any kind of work. One day I was busy doing repairs, and I thought my father was napping. Wrong! He was busy removing the hardware from the only bathroom we had with a shower. It took my husband a while to get it back in working condition before he could clean up after working all day long.

There was one other time my father thought he would lend a helping hand. He was napping when I looked in on him. "Oh good, all is well." I had a few minutes, so I started painting the baseboards in the kitchen. All was still very quiet; I heard no noise for a very long time. Finally up from his nap, my father came down the hall, and I put the paint away (no explanation needed, right?). Later that night, the breakers kept going off. We had no idea what the cause of this new annoyance was, but my husband searched the house and could find nothing out of the ordinary or a reason for what was happening, so we called an electrician to the tune of big bucks. The electrician was shocked with his findings. My father had rewired the outlets in his room in such a manner that he could have been electrocuted. I still don't know where he found the tools to do all this extra work. I made a mental note to myself: all quiet times must be checked into immediately.

We had a security system installed before we moved in the house. I just needed to be on the alert if my father left the house. I did not stop him from going out, but I did need to know when he had left the building, so to speak. He often thought it was time to go to work or church and constantly looked for his car, telling me he could not remember where he had parked it.

When he decided to take off walking, I would follow him in my car until I thought he was tired enough to agree to let me take him home. I would ask him if he wanted a ride, and he would say, "Yes." He would get in the car, and we would go home. He always asked me how I knew where he lived, or he might even try to pay me.

I never knew who I was going to be next with him. Once he said, "I wish you would have known my wife. I think you would have loved her."

My heartfelt reply was, "Yes, you are right, I think I would have."

Once we were walking down the hall of the veterans' hospital, and before we reached our destination, I was my mother, my sister and me in the same conversation. He asked me, "How many children do we have?" I answered him truthfully, saying four girls.

Then there were countless times that he would complain about me to me. This just makes me smile with a sad heart at the same time, if that is possible. He said to me, "The lady that runs this place is mean!" I asked him why he thought she was mean, and his reply was, "She makes me eat stuff I don't like, and I have to take a bath."

I told him, "If that lady ever gives you any more problems, you just let me know, and I will make her be nice to you."

He said, "Okay, I'll do that." He thought my husband and I were the gardener and the maid! I still laugh about that! In a way, he was correct.

My father had been rushed to the hospital more than once by way of ambulance, and the many trips for doctor's appointments had just become a way of life for us. We had to keep a sense of humor, or it would have been just too unbearable.

Then came the day. I knew it would happen; he just sat there staring, unable to talk. We called the ambulance, and back to the veterans' hospital he went. He was kept for observation, and he kept the place hopping. The hospital ended up having to assign a nurse to stay with him around the clock. They said he needed 24-hour care and asked if I had anyone to help care for him at home. I told them no, I did not. That is when we were told he needed more care than I could give and needed to be placed in a long-term care facility.

I had to sign my father (the one who trusted me to care for him) into a nursing home. I had to convince him to sign his name on the very piece of paper that was going to keep him from coming home with me. I had to look at the expression on his face when he got up to go with me when I had to leave, but he didn't get to come me. I will never forget that look. Did I know this was the best thing for him? Yes, I knew that. Did it make him or me feel better about the situation? NO. It was just more than either one of us could deal with at the moment though. I cried my heart out for months, feeling as though I had betrayed the trust he had placed in me. Was he thinking I had abandoned him too? "OH, DEAR HEAVENLY FATHER, I HOPE NOT."

He took on a new career upon entering the string of nursing homes he would have to stay in over that last two and one-half years of his life: being an escape artist. In the very first facility, he broke the security code and made his way out of the building, and he would have gotten away, but he stopped to help his friends get over the fence too. Each was lured back with the promise of a peanut butter and jelly sandwich. At the second facility, I warned the staff of his unique abilities, and they assured me would not break their code or escape. However, he honed his skills and escaped from there, too, and continued to break out every chance he got, no matter how secure the building. For the most part, he would go by himself, and if he was not caught in the act, he would be found in a local church.

Once when I returned home from church, there was a phone message saying my father was still missing, for now going on the fifth hour, but not to worry—the police were on the lookout for him. I found no comfort in any part of that message. Then when a local church called the police to say there was a man sitting in the church who wouldn't leave, we knew it had to be him. He had gotten dressed for church and walked out like he knew where he was going. He had to cross some very busy streets and walk a very long distance to get to the church in which they found him. I promptly took him out of that place, too.

Then, the next inevitable stage showed up. He could no longer talk, swallowing was very difficult, and he was choking with almost every bite of food he was given because he no longer remembered how to feed himself. His general health was declining at a fast and steady pace. He was wheelchair bound, sat most of the time with a blank stare fixed on his face, and recognized not one single person. But he continued to struggle for his freedom. As he struggled, he managed to hurt himself, mostly by falling, either by trying to get out of bed or by trying to walk in his own strength. In many ways, I knew how he felt. I struggled to get away from the bondage in my life, too. I just had to keep reminding myself that the truth is what makes you free, and the truth was, I could not escape the bondage in my life in my own strength either. It was only by the grace of God that I did not quit.

Chapter 8

Can You Wait a Minute, Lord? I Have to Dust!

Slow obedience is no obedience, and my Father in Heaven is no different than my father on earth was in that respect. When my father told me to do something, he expected it to be done in the manner he instructed and when he wanted it done—not when I felt like doing it. That, of course, was for my own good. That was such a hard lesson for me to learn, and I really did not understand the concept until I had children of my own; then I really understood. I, too, expected my children to obey immediately. I still struggle with that from time to time. When things look impossible or too overwhelming for me (like writing this book), I will put them off as long as I can. I think back to when my father was the designated executor of his stepfather's will. If he would have just followed his stepfather's instructions instead of handing that difficult task over to his demanding mother, the promises would have been fulfilled. He ended up blaming others for his lack when really it was all due to his lack of obedience. Our Father in Heaven cannot and will not break His promises to us, but we must do our part with immediate obedience.

I am so sorry; I have neglected to introduce myself. I'm a sinner, saved by "God's grace." ***Ephesians 2:8, 9*** says, ***"For by grace are ye saved through faith; and that not of yourselves: it is the gift of God: Not of works, lest any man should boast."*** So, there you have it. The truth is out. The rest of the news is, I will be a sinner until the day I die. And my sins do continually beset me.

There is hope, though, because God will not stop the pruning until then either. As I ask God to use me, He always picks things for me to do for which I am unqualified. I still have to call upon ***Philippians 4:13***, that is for sure: ***"I can do all things through Christ which strengtheneth me."***

Prayer is a very powerful tool. God ultimately does the rest. I find myself praying more in the difficult times of my life than in the resting times. I always want to make sure my requests are "of God's will" and not of my wants or wishes. There was a time when I felt a prompting to change churches. Well, this of course had to be Satan because God would never put me in a perfectly good church and prompt me to leave it, would He?

Proverbs 3:5 came to mind after the fact. You know, that part about, ***"...lean not on your own understanding."*** Well, who knew? That prompting came a second time! I didn't get it that time either. Then God fixed it so I couldn't miss it the third time around. An event took place in our very own home. A person from the church we were attending came over uninvited, but welcome just the same. Thinking he was going to be of help, he began to say things about which he did not have all the facts. This person, one we trusted, made some inaccurate accusations, said more things, and got rather loud. Our trust bond was broken right then and there. WOW, how quickly things can get out of control when a person doesn't know what he is talking about and is not willing to listen to all the facts. The situation only gets worse when the trouble maker could have set things straight but chooses, for his pride sake, to remain silent and thus guiltless in the eyes of man.

A friend of mine told me about a young preacher starting a church in the city in which she lived. I listened, but it concerned me not. (Again, with hindsight in my favor, that was the first introduction to the church where God was going to send us.) Then our son recommended we try the same church my friend had told me about. Well, I told my son, I wanted to go to a church in the city in which I lived, not one I would have to drive 15 miles to attend. I wanted to be active and attend everything, and I thought that was way too far to drive. I cannot even believe I said those words, but I did. I regretted them as soon as they were out of my mouth. I had read the Bible so many times and knew that Jesus was willing to do all for me. He had walked willingly to the Cross to die for my sins. Now here I was, complaining about driving a few miles in the car He had so graciously supplied for me. This just proves how human (ungrateful) I am. I saw that, repented immediately, and we went the following Sunday in March of 1996. My husband and I both knew this was the church God would have us attend.

Has this ever happened to you? You were asked to do something, and you really didn't want to do it, or you were busy doing something else and wanted to finish that project before you got started on anything new? Well, my hand is raised right now, too. That has happened so many times to me. I have to confess, as you will see, that I have handed out my share and more of excuses as to why I wouldn't, couldn't or shouldn't, and all of them to the LORD. Remember Him? He was the One Who willingly died for me on the Cross. The One Who paid for my sins, the One Who forgave me once and for all, the One Whom I can call at any time, night or day, and He is never too busy for me. It's He I am talking about; He is the One for Whom I can't find time. Isn't that gratitude at its finest? It's a lousy shame at it's worst—that's what it is!

When we started attending this new church, there were very few people, and I said I was willing to do what I could to help. I was still dealing with my father, and MY FATHER in Heaven was still dealing with me. It was a real strain on life in general—mentally, physically, and on my marriage. But I was still in it for the long haul. I do not want to give anyone a false impression. I have needed the grace of God more than anyone in this story. I am not without flaw or claw. A person can only dig at me so long before I start digging back, and sometimes it is with revenge. (That is just in case you hadn't noticed prior to this proclamation.) Have I gotten away with it? NO, I haven't. The people and the LORD catch up with me every single time. Am I bragging or making excuses? NO, I am just keeping the record straight, sinner that I am.

I was asked to do more things in this new church. Most of it I did not want to do because I was still busy with my father and I was flat worn out. But Christ did not offer up any excuses when He died for me, so I took on whatever was asked of me, but not without difficulty, I might add. There was every opposition you can imagine. I said I was willing to serve the Lord under any and all circumstances and was put to the test. To save time and all the boring details, I'll list a few of the many obstacles I had to hurdle in order to still serve. There were difficulties that included the patch on one eye as a result of having a wart removed from my eyelid (I do thank God it was not located on the end of my nose or on my chin, with long black hairs growing out of it, like some thought it should have been), a swollen face from dental work gone bad, and a cast on one foot from tripping over someone. Then there were the headaches and blurred vision as a result of the concussion I got in the first of several car accidents, not to mention the agony I suffered from the back pain. Did I mention that I cannot take pain medication?

Then, there were the heartaches. Yes, the heartaches were the worst to deal with, I think. There is a song in the *Soul Stirring Songs & Hymns* book titled "Stand Up, Stand Up for Jesus," by George J. Webb. The third verse says, "The arm of flesh will fail you, Ye dare not trust your own." And it is so true. We have to put our trust in Jesus and Him alone; we dare not trust ourselves.

There is no pain medication for the heartaches others (intentionally or unintentionally) inflict upon us or for the ones we inflict upon ourselves, not to mention the pain we cause others. People will always be a source of pain to us, and those closest to us will be the ones who hurt us the most. But, **"...*love covereth all sins,*"** the Bible says in the last part of **Proverbs 10:12.**

Taking care of my father was the hardest thing I have ever had to do. I hated seeing what the loss of his mind had brought him through. He had never given up on me, and I am so glad God gave me the grace to not give up on him. I have no regrets, and I would do it again. It truly took faith for me to continue caring for my father because it just looked so impossible. I was so tired mentally and physically, but in my heart I could not quit. When my father was instructing me on how to drive in the snow, even though the situation looked extremely impossible, I followed his instruction not knowing if I could really depend on him or not because of his dementia. I followed his instructions explicitly, even though it didn't look like I should or could trust him. I trusted him, and it worked out perfectly. Even though God is prompting us to do something that looks impossible, He will get us through it if we just follow His instructions. Remember **Hebrews 11:1, *"Now faith is the substance of things hoped for, the evidence of things not seen."***

When my father went to be with the LORD, on November 1, 2000, I was not by his side. I was glad the Lord spared me that moment. After all we had been through the preceding six and one-half years, it just might have been more than I could have borne. It was such sweet sorrow. Knowing he would no longer have to struggle for anything was the sweet part, and the fact that he was gone from this earth was to my sorrow. I have missed him so much. I do take comfort in **Revelation 21:4, *"And God shall wipe away all tears from their eyes; and there shall be no more death, neither sorrow, nor crying, neither shall there be any more pain: for the former things are passed away."***

My father on earth and my Father in Heaven wait for me in Heaven, while I continue to run the race with patience, the race that is set before me, while looking unto Jesus, the One Who has prepared a place for me, my advocate, the author and finisher of my faith, Who is sitting at the right hand of the throne of God. I know that to be true because He said so in **John 14:2, 3, *"In my Father's house are many mansions: if it were not so, I would have told you. I go to prepare a place for you. And if I go and prepare a place for you, I will come again, and receive you unto myself; that where I am, there ye may be also."***

So here we are many years later. Am I the virtuous woman? Nope, not yet. Will I ever be? Only God knows the answer to that, but it is a goal to set before me. Are all my heart- aches gone? Nope, not yet, but the Lord will be there with me giving me the grace to get through each one of them and, hopefully, with a smile in my heart if not on my face. If I have learned anything at all as a Christian, the unsaved will never want the God I have if I'm not happy with Him. Well, I am happy with Him. I just have to remind myself from time to time to let Him be Who He needs to be, to make me be who I need to be for Christ's sake. After all, I am not my own. I was bought with the price, that being Christ's blood that was shed on the Cross at Calvary.

By the grace of God, my husband and I still sit next to each other in church. We are serving the Lord side by side in the church our third son and his wife started. We are all growing in grace together.

And I say, Amen to that.

www.ingramcontent.com/pod-product-compliance
Ingram Content Group UK Ltd.
Pitfield, Milton Keynes, MK11 3LW, UK
UKHW041948230426
12048UKWH00008B/214